CONOR McPHERSON

Conor McPherson was born in Dublin in 1971 and attended University College Dublin, where he began to write and direct. Original stage plays include *Rum & Vodka*, *The Good Thief*, *This Lime Tree Bower*, *St Nicholas*, *The Weir* (Olivier, Evening Standard and Critics Circle Awards), *Dublin Carol*, *Port Authority*, *Shining City* (Tony Award-nominated), *The Seafarer* (Tony, Olivier and Evening Standard Award nominations), *The Veil* and *The Night Alive* (New York Drama Critics' Circle Award for Best Play). His 2020 adaptation of Chekhov's *Uncle Vanya* won the South Bank Show Sky Arts Theatre Award and was broadcast by BBC TV and PBS in the United States.

His collaboration with Bob Dylan, *Girl from the North Country*, opened at The Old Vic, London, before transferring to the West End (winning two Olivier Awards) and Broadway, where it was nominated for seven Tony Awards, including Best Musical, Best Director, Best Book of a Musical, and won the Tony for Best Orchestrations.

Awards for his screenwriting include four Best Screenplay Awards from the Irish Film and Television Academy; Spanish Screenwriters' Circle Best Screenplay Award; the CICAE award for Best Film from the Berlin Film Festival; the Jury Prize from the San Sebastián Film Festival; and the Méliès d'argent award for Best European Film.

ELVIS COSTELLO

Elvis Costello is a writer and musician who made several records in the twentieth century, many of which are still remembered today. He is the composer of thirty-five record albums, over five hundred published titles, including fifteen songs co-written with Paul McCartney and notable collaborations with Burt Bacharach, Allen Toussaint, the Brodsky Quartet, T Bone Burnett and Diana Krall.

Elvis's songs have been recorded by Roy Orbison, Chet Baker and Johnny Cash. He has written lyrics for the music of Billy Strayhorn, twelve Charles Mingus compositions and the score for an adaptation of Budd Schulberg's *A Face in the Crowd*, as well as setting a dozen unpublished lyrics by Bob Dylan. He is a member of both the Songwriters Hall of Fame and the Rock and Roll Hall of Fame, holding two honorary doctorates in music.

Conor McPherson

COLD WAR

A stage version of the film by
Paweł Pawlikowski

Music by
Elvis Costello

NICK HERN BOOKS
London
www.nickhernbooks.co.uk

A Nick Hern Book

Cold War first published in 2023 by Nick Hern Books Limited, The Glasshouse, 49a Goldhawk Road, London W12 8QP

Cover image: © Maksim_Selin/iStock

Designed and typeset by Nick Hern Books, London
Printed in the UK by Mimeo Ltd, Huntingdon, Cambridgeshire PE29 6XX

A CIP catalogue record for this book is available from the British Library

ISBN   978 1 83904 309 3

www.nickhernbooks.co.uk/environmental-policy

Cold War was first performed at the Almeida Theatre, London, on 30 November 2023, with the following cast:

ZULA	Anya Chalotra
DANCE CAPTAIN/ENSEMBLE	Ali Goldsmith
ENSEMBLE	Ryan Goscinski
VICE CONSUL	Elliot Harper
KACZMAREK	Elliot Levey
ENSEMBLE	Ediz Mahmut
JULIETTE/ANIA	Anastasia Martin
ENSEMBLE	Alžbeta Matyšáková
MICHEL/MINISTER	Jordan Metcalfe
AIMEE/ENSEMBLE	Katarina Novkovic
WIKTOR	Luke Thallon
ENSEMBLE	Sophie Maria Wojna
IRENA	Alex Young

Book	Conor McPherson
Music	Elvis Costello
Original Film	Paweł Pawlikowski
Director	Rupert Goold
Music Supervisor, Orchestrations and Arrangements	Simon Hale
Choreographer	Ellen Kane
Set Designer	Jon Bausor
Costume Designer	Evie Gurney
Lighting Designer	Paule Constable
Sound Designer	Sinéad Diskin
Musical Director	Jo Cichonska
Orchestral Management	David Gallagher
Casting Director	Amy Ball CDG
Costume Supervisor	Peter Todd
Wigs, Hair and Make-up Supervisor	Moira O'Connell
Assistant Director	Dubheasa Lanipekun
Associate Choreographer	James Cousins
Music Assistant	Manuel Pestana Gageiro
Associate Costume Designer	Phoebe Shu-Ching Chan
Associate Musical Director	Livi van Warmelo
Copyist	James Humphreys
Sound Associate	Bryony Blackler
Folk Music Consultants	Warsaw Village Band
Language Coach	Edyta Nowosielska
Dialect Coach	Fabien Enjalric
Folk Dance Consultants	Orleta

6

Characters

~~WIKTOR, *a pianist, composer and arranger*~~
ZULA, *a singer and dancer*
IRENA, *a musicologist, teacher and archivist*
KACZMAREK, *a state-employed administrator*
MICHEL, *a music producer*
JULIETTE, *a writer*
AIMEE, *a singer*
ANIA, *a young singer*
DELIA, *a film producer*
HERBERT, *a film producer*
MICHEL, *a music producer*

And STATE OFFICIALS, SINGERS, DANCERS, WAITERS, BOHEMIANS, PRISON GUARDS, SOLDIERS, *a* NANNY

Setting

Poland, Berlin, Paris, 1949–1964.

The scenes can move fluidly from place to place with a minimum of set/props.

Note on Text

Words in square brackets are unspoken.

This text went to press before the end of rehearsals and so may differ slightly from the play as performed.

ACT ONE

Poland, winter 1949.

In the darkness a voice rings out singing 'At My Mother's House':

GIRL.
U Moje Matecki brzunkali slunecki
A tero nie bendo bo ni ma corecki
Oj-la-la-la, oj-la-la-la
Oj-la-la-la, oj-la-la-la

Instrumental verse.

Brzunkajta sklunecki jekiesta brzunkali
Kochajta me chlopcy jekiesta kochali

CHORUS.
Oj-la-la-la, oj-la-la-la
Oj-la-la-la, oj-la-la-la
Oj-la-la-la, oj-la-la-la
Oj-la-la-la, oj-la-la-la

Lights rise on a cold village hall in a little rural town.

WIKTOR and IRENA *stand listening to two* GIRLS *singing this song.* WIKTOR *has headphones on, attached to a reel-to-reel recording device, holding a microphone out towards the music.*

IRENA *makes notes in a logbook.*

GIRL.
Oj-la-la-la, oj-la-la-la
Oj-la-la-la, oj-la-la-la
Oj-la-la-la, oj-la-la-la
Oj-la-la-la, oj-la-la-la

KACZMAREK *stamps up and down, bored, flapping his arms to stay warm. He stops the performance.*

KACZMAREK. All right, thank you!

He ushers the GIRLS *out.*

IRENA. What?

KACZMAREK. I've heard that song about fifteen fucking times today – everywhere we go! Too crude. They're all too crude.

IRENA. That's the mountain style.

KACZMAREK. Style my arse. Where I come from – every drunk sings like that.

A MAN WITH A HURDY-GURDY *starts to audition…*

HURDY-GURDY PLAYER.
Oj-la-la-la, oj-la-la-la
Oj-la-la-la, oj-la-la-la
Oj-la-la-la, oj-la-la-la
Oj-la-la-la, oj-la-la-la

KACZMAREK. What the hell are we doing out here? Let's go back.

IRENA. We can't go back. We have three more villages to…

KACZMAREK. No. I've had enough. I need a drink. Anyway – the sun's going down. The roads'll be black ice in an hour.

IRENA. Then let me drive.

KACZMAREK (*looks at* WIKTOR *for support*). You drive? With respect, my dear, I'm not sure you'd be able to manage our truck.

IRENA. Why not?

KACZMAREK. Look, I'll be honest with you – when I *don't* drive, I get anxious. Out here in the middle of nowhere, in the dark – with you driving, you're tired, you've been up since the crack of dawn, one false gear shift, we end up in a ditch, having to stay the night in some little cottage? With some huge extended family and the old granny crouching there staring at us? I mean purely even on an existential level…

ZULA (*interrupting*). Is this the auditions?

They turn to see a young woman standing in the doorway.

KACZMAREK. No, we're finished. No more today.

ZULA. What?! I've been standing out here in the snow for two hours!

KACZMAREK. Anyway, we're not doing auditions. That's next week.

ZULA. So, what are you doing?

IRENA. Collecting music.

ZULA. What music?

IRENA. Folk music.

KACZMAREK. Don't tell her anything. Polish music.

ZULA. I have folk music. I know hundreds of songs.

KACZMAREK. But you haven't even auditioned.

ZULA. That's why I'm here. Tell me what to sing!

KACZMAREK. We haven't finished collecting the songs!

ZULA. So collect my songs!

KACZMAREK. We'll do it at the auditions!

ZULA. When are the auditions?!

KACZMAREK. When we've finished collecting the songs!

ZULA. All right, keep your wig on. Where do you want me to stand?

KACZMAREK. Outside! I told you – we're finished for today.

IRENA. What's your name?

ZULA (*to* IRENA). Zuzanna Lichón. Zula.

KACZMAREK (*with genial finality*). You're not on the list.

ZULA. What list?

KACZMAREK *waves* IRENA *and* WIKTOR *out.*

KACZMAREK. The list is irrelevant because we've had technical difficulties! We have three more towns to visit today!

WIKTOR *and* IRENA *head out.*

ZULA. I paid to get here. I have to pay to get back.

KACZMAREK. From where?

ZULA. Murzasichle.

KACZMAREK. Moorza-what-icle?

ZULA. Murzasichle.

KACZMAREK. Where the hell is that?

ZULA. I gave a lorry driver thirty-five zloty to get here.

KACZMAREK. I'm not giving you thirty-five zloty! Come here.

ZULA *stands in front of him. He looks at her.*

Turn around.

She does so. He looks her up and down.

(*Suddenly relenting, giving her a ticket.*) All right, here, take it.

ZULA. What is it?

KACZMAREK. For the auditions. It's next week. Just you. And don't tell anyone. All right? You're welcome.

He goes. Voices sing underscore…

ENSEMBLE.
The devil knocked three times
I opened up my door
'I'll give you anything you want'
'My lover's heart is all'

'That deal is easy done,' he swore
He held me with a grin
But when the time has come to pay
You better let me in

Giant windows of a dilapidated ballroom come into focus as the village hall melts away. Sunlight rises in the windows. A table full of food is laid out against one wall.

A dozen young SINGERS *and* DANCERS *come in to where* KACZMAREK, WIKTOR *and* IRENA *wait. The young folk wear dishevelled old clothes.* ZULA *is among the group.*

They continue singing under KACZMAREK's *welcome speech.*

KACZMAREK. Young friends! You may be wondering what you are doing here, in this stately house. Well, thanks to the beneficence of our esteemed leaders, should you prove yourselves worthy, this may just become your home. Through this door you enter a world of music, song and dance – Irena?

IRENA. Yes, our remit is to find performers for our national music.

KACZMAREK. The music of pain and humiliation…

IRENA. And joy and celebration too.

KACZMAREK. And joy – yes, of course. Like you, yes, I've laughed at some of these old folk songs from the fields, from the mountains – didn't think much of them – why? Because they originated in the minds of an uneducated proletariat? Because they're not as elevated as the so-called bourgeois 'classics'? Well, nobody's laughing now – are they, Irena?

IRENA. No.

KACZMAREK. Because this is the music of victory! You may be wondering: will everyone be allowed through this door? And my answer is: absolutely not. Our government has decreed that only the very cream of our young talent will be permitted to remain. And under the careful supervision of our tutors, Irena Komorowska, and our musical director here, Wiktor Zatoński – should you be accepted, you will rehearse and work and strive to become an elite troupe – to perform on our country's great stages. To inspire our people – to express what has been subjugated and lain buried for too long within their souls. So, I invite you now, today, to join the fierce and noble struggle with yourselves and with each other for our limited places. Successful auditionees will be given clean clothes, three meals a day, medical check-ups and unlimited political instruction. So good luck to you all. Hurrah!

The group ravenously attacks the table of food, breaking into little huddles, stuffing their faces. Some take their food outside. WIKTOR *and* IRENA *set up a work table at one end of the room.*

ZULA *joins a girl,* ANIA, *and* BOY *at the other end of the room. She speaks through her stuffed mouth as she devours a sandwich.*

ZULA. Do we have to be able to read music?

BOY. Nah. Someone said they want it peasant-style. Whatever that is.

ANIA. Songs from the radio?

BOY. No – old songs. Too shit for the radio.

He takes his food, stuffing some extra up his sweater, and heads out into the sunshine.

ZULA *turns to* ANIA.

ZULA. What will you sing?

ANIA. Just a song we used to sing in school. You?

ZULA. Don't know yet. How does it go, this tune of yours?

ANIA *considers* ZULA.

You can trust me, I'm not going to steal it!

ANIA *starts singing 'Hej Sokoły':*

ANIA.
'See there by the black water...'

ZULA Everybody knows that one! It would be nice with two
voices. Start again.

ZULA joins in with a low harmony. ANIA nods.

ZULA *and* ANIA.
See there by the black water
A handsome soldier sits on horseback
While his true love stands beside him
Crying for his safe return-o
Hey, hey fly the falcons...

*Hearing them, WIKTOR stops working. He stands at the
table.*

WIKTOR. Girls. Please.

*WIKTOR motions them to the table. IRENA continues
working, getting the ledgers out, she's not ready to start
auditions. She casts a cold eye on WIKTOR.*

Go on.

*ZULA and ANIA start their song again. They harmonise
beautifully, mesmerising WIKTOR.*

ANIA *and* ZULA.
Hey, hey fly the falcons
Over mountains forests and valleys
Ring ring ring the church bells
Bring my lover home to me-o...

IRENA. Thank you. After delousing, we'll call you – as per
your numbers – when we are ready to start.

The GIRLS turn to leave.

WIKTOR. What else have you got?

ZULA. To sing?

WIKTOR. Yes.

*ZULA starts to sing a song, 'Serdtse' from the 1934 movie
Jolly Fellows.*

ZULA.

Kak mnogo laskovykh imyon
No lish'odno iz nikh trevozhit
Unosya pokoy i son
Kak mnogo devushek khoroshikh
Kak mnogo laskovykh imyon
No lish'odno iz nikh trevozhit
Unosya pokoy i son kogda vlyublyon

IRENA. Thank you.

ZULA. And the chorus!

(*Singing.*) Foolish heart, you never about contentment
Foolish heart, it's so great to be alive!
Foolish heart, I am so grateful that you're like this
Oh thank you, foolish heart, for showing me the pain of love!

ZULA *finishes.* WIKTOR *is bewitched.* IRENA *is peeved.*

WIKTOR. Russian song? Where did you get it?

ZULA. The movies.

WIKTOR. How's your dancing?

ZULA. I know the basic moves. The rest I can learn.

She puts her fists on her hips, does a few stamps to the left and right.

This kind of thing, right?

IRENA. Yes, we'll call your number when we get started.
Thank you.

ZULA. Thank you.

ZULA *and* ANIA *leave the audition room.*

IRENA *watches as* WIKTOR *writes in his ledger.*

IRENA (*continues getting her stuff ready*). The other one had
a beautiful, pure traditional voice.

WIKTOR. But that one has something too.

IRENA Mm?

WIKTOR. Energy. Spirit. She's original.

IRENA. But we're not looking for 'original', Wiktor, are we?

WIKTOR. I suppose.

IRENA. Anyway, she's up to something. She's not from Murzasichle. She's from Łódź. Having us all on.

WIKTOR. She sings well.

IRENA. She did time too.

WIKTOR. What?

IRENA. Stabbed her own father with a bread knife. They locked her up in a hospital. She's on a suspended sentence.

WIKTOR. Who told you?

IRENA. Kaczmarek had her checked her out. Everybody gets checked out, Wiktor. This is for the fatherland, you know – not for us.

WIKTOR *playfully pretends to give* IRENA *a kick up the backside. She yelps and darts away, enjoying his attention. She suddenly folds herself into his arms.*

What?

WIKTOR. Nothing.

WIKTOR *smiles reassuringly and kisses her on the forehead. But* IRENA *sees nothing sincere in his eyes.*

IRENA. Oh Wiktor. (*She turns away and calls out.*) Right! Numbers one, five, nine and six!

Music.

The troupe is practising a traditional dance with IRENA. *They laugh as they sing a traditional song, getting the steps wrong. They have to keeping stopping and starting.* IRENA *watches as* ZULA *picks a better dancing partner for herself.*

The lights change to…

Afternoon. ZULA *arrives for her singing lesson with* WIKTOR.

WIKTOR *has lyrics and manuscripts scattered all over the floor. He is on his knees trying to organise them.*

ZULA. Hello. I'm sorry. Were you praying?

WIKTOR. What? Oh sorry no. I'm just trying to organise all these songs into some kind of system.

ZULA. How's it going?

WIKTOR. Well, there's a rough map now. Love songs here. Songs about the devil here. More love songs. More devil songs. And one song over here that seems to be about a large talking pig who's also a kind of hairdresser.

ZULA. I know that one!

WIKTOR. Really?

ZULA. Yes!

WIKTOR. Right I'll…

ZULA. They said you wanted to hear my range?

WIKTOR. No, yes. Can you try this?

He plays a few arpeggios which she sings back to him with almost perfect pitch.

He plays something a bit more complicated, becoming… a snatch of his own composition, 'I Do'. ZULA *copies the melody. She even improvises a little.* WIKTOR *is impressed.*

ZULA. You play well.

WIKTOR *doesn't answer, just keeps playing.*

You're too good for this. You should be playing in an orchestra somewhere.

WIKTOR. Like where?

ZULA. I don't know. Paris? New York?

WIKTOR *smiles*.

Who taught you to play?

WIKTOR. I studied composition at Warsaw. Where did you learn all the songs we're doing?

ZULA. My dad made me and my sisters sing in the tenement courtyards for money but I used to sneak off into the church – they had an organ you could pump with your feet.

WIKTOR. Your sisters didn't want to audition?

ZULA. No. They're… They were…

WIKTOR. Oh, I'm sorry.

ZULA. What were you playing there? That you made me sing – just now.

He plays some of 'I Do (Zula's Theme)'.

Yes. What is that?

WIKTOR. Nothing. Something I've been working on. In my spare…

ZULA. You composed that?

He shrugs.

We should do it.

WIKTOR. It's not a folk song.

ZULA. Does it have lyrics?

WIKTOR (*shakes his head*). I don't… [*write lyrics.*]

ZULA picks up some lyrics from the pile on the piano.

ZULA (*sings, improvising*).
There's a tree at the crossroads
There's a nail in my shoe
Repeat to me softly
As you vow that we'll see it through…

WIKTOR plays along with her, introducing interesting classical chords. She smiles as she sings.

> Let's go to the other side
> And take in the view
> Our eyes will see better there
> Watching the river flow
> You may say I don't know, but I do…
>
> Now your turn.

WIKTOR. No, I don't sing.

ZULA. Well then, speak-sing.

WIKTOR (*tries singing, ends up coughing*).
   Every night…
   (*Coughs.*) Sorry.
   (*Tries singing.*) Will be starless…

ZULA. No, go on, go again.

WIKTOR. I can't sing…

   (*Sings.*) Every night will be starless…
   Every day will be fine…

WIKTOR *and* ZULA.
   Each hour will be peaceful
   As the reeds make the river slow…

   The earth will be broken…

   And we'll lie there alone
   I am yours you are mine
   To long for longer is a crime
   You may say I don't lie
   But I do, but I do…

   Something has happened between them in this moment. They look at each other in silence.

ZULA. It's nice. Use those. (*She writes the lyrics down.*)

WIKTOR. It's six o' clock. You'll be late for political instruction.

ZULA (*mock alarm*). Oh my God! My politics! What will I do?

   ZULA *darts out the door.*

WIKTOR sits silently. He plays a little more of 'I Do'. Then the lights change to dusk and he starts to play Chopin's 'Nocturne in B flat minor, Op. 9 no. 1'.

In a half-finished dressing room, IRENA is fitting folk costumes with two older SEAMSTRESSES on to two of the GIRLS.

Wrapped in their blankets, ZULA and two GIRLS sit on the windowsill, listening to WIKTOR's playing at the open window, the night breeze playing with their hair.

Two GIRLS get up and start to silently dance to the music...

IRENA comes to WIKTOR and sits with him, her head on his shoulder. But there is something remote about him – unavailable.

KACZMAREK comes in and stands listening to the music, a bottle of clear liquor in his hand. He finds a couple of cups and pours drinks.

KACZMAREK. What is that?

IRENA. Chopin.

KACZMAREK. Of course. I knew that. You nervous at all?
    About our big debut – in front of the minister – on Saturday?

IRENA. Nerves are good. They'll keep us sharp.

KACZMAREK. I'm already too sharp. I had to find something
    to take the edge off. The minister will want to see what he's
    spent all this money on and if it's not up to scratch it'll be me
    that gets the – (*He mimes a pistol shooting someone.*) We
    will be ready, won't we?

IRENA. We'll be ready.

KACZMAREK. This is distilled from old rotten potatoes.
    (*Retching from the liquor.*) Fucking hell. Oof. You have to
    hand it to our people. The ingenuity of local folk knowledge.
    Passed down from father to son to grandson and great-
    grandson and before you know it every single generation is
    nicely sozzled – staring at you, cross-eyed. We used to make

this kind of... wine. Made it from these bunches of buttercups grew round our camp. In the war. It was disgusting. Tasted like alcoholic urine. The Hungarian guards let us drink it 'cause it kept us quiet. Where were you, Wiktor?

WIKTOR. Hm?

KACZMAREK. In the war. Abroad?

WIKTOR. No. Warsaw.

KACZMAREK. Warsaw? For the whole war?

IRENA. He was teaching.

KACZMAREK. Essential work, I suppose. Teaching. You studied under the great Magdalena Abrahamson, didn't you?

WIKTOR. Abramowicz.

KACZMAREK. Magdalena Abramowicz.

IRENA. He taught languages.

KACZMAREK. What language? German? I'm joking. I don't care what you did. You wouldn't believe some of the shit I did. I had no idea you were so well-known.

WIKTOR. I'm not well-known.

KACZMAREK. Oh no, some higher-ups were here this morning, and they were very interested to know who you were, yes. Here. (*He produces bundles of coupons from his pockets.*) They gave us some coupons... Go on. Take 'em! But make sure you sign the back – you see – under my signature. Co-sign. Co-signatories. And don't tell anyone. You're not supposed to have these. We all look after each other, right? That's... I mean, otherwise...

KACZMAREK *shrugs and goes.* IRENA *sits with* WIKTOR *in silence.*

The moon shines down on them all... the light changes to morning as the tempo quickens and the easy playful dance to Chopin becomes a febrile rehearsal, with IRENA *knocking the troupe into shape, some in half-finished costumes, some in completed costumes.*

BOYS *and* GIRLS *move across the room in twos – the* GIRLS *helping the* BOYS *in a wild, half-cartwheel spin.* IRENA *shouts instructions. She whacks a dancer with a stick.*

IRENA. Leg higher!

The next pair take their turn.

Good.

And the next. Beautiful, Mateusz, bravo!

BOYS *and* GIRLS *spin and twirl across the room, dancing an oberek.* IRENA *claps for them, shouting at them to:*

Keep to the tempo! Look at each other!

They've all come a long way since their arrival. Smiling, WIKTOR *watches* ZULA *from his usual spot at the piano.*

One two three one two three – Hook!! And turn!

The lights change. Everything goes quiet. We hear an orchestra tuning up.

The troupe line up behind a curtain waiting to perform in a hall. They stretch and warm up their voices.

We hear the hum of an audience waiting for the show; chatter and shuffling about, some background music.

IRENA *goes along the line, fixing their costumes, making sure they are ready.*

WIKTOR *paces up and down anxiously.*

ZULA. You're going to wear a hole in the stage.

WIKTOR. Sorry?

ZULA. Walking up and down like that.

WIKTOR. Oh. Am I? I didn't... [*realise.*]

ZULA. Nervous?

WIKTOR. No. I just can't swallow for some reason.

ZULA. Probably just nerves.

WIKTOR. Mm.

ZULA. How many people are out there?

WIKTOR. Eight hundred, a thousand, something like that.

ZULA. Not so bad. It's good! To have an audience!

WIKTOR. Mm... It's just there's a lot riding on... you know... tonight. You nervous?

ZULA. I can swallow. I'm fine. Why would I get nervous?

WIKTOR. 'Cause it's normal.

ZULA. So you're normal. Listen to me. I'm not going to let you down. You can have full confidence in me.

WIKTOR (*laughs*). Alright.

ZULA. Don't laugh at me!

WIKTOR. I'm not laughing at you.

ZULA. You'll be laughing on the other side of your face after this.

WIKTOR. I know. I do have confidence in you.

ZULA. You sure?

WIKTOR. Yes, no I'm... it's not you. You're amazing, really. I'm just...

ZULA. I think *you* are. You're amazing. So don't worry.

> ZULA *grabs* WIKTOR*'s hand, gives it a quick reassuring squeeze and lets go as* IRENA *comes to them.*

IRENA. All right?

WIKTOR. Yep.

IRENA. First positions. Good luck, everybody!

> *The troupe assemble themselves into a choir. The curtain rises.*

> ZULA *and* ANIA *sing the first verse of 'Pid Oblaczkom' – with amended lyrics – at the head of the choir.*

WIKTOR *is in the orchestra pit, dressed in a dark suit and bow tie, conducting the troupe.*

ZULA *and* ANIA *(singing).*
The devil knocked three times
I opened up my door
'I'll give you anything you want'
'My lover's heart is all'

'That deal is easy done' he swore
He held me with a grin
'But when the time has come to pay
You better let me in'

WIKTOR *brings in the rest of the* ENSEMBLE.

ENSEMBLE.
'You better let me in,' he said
'For no one knows the cold
Like one who's been cast down alone
Their story never told'

I said my word was true
My obligations would I meet
I swore on the bones of my family
That lay beneath our feet
Our family
Beneath our feet

WIKTOR *turns to the audience and the troupe all take their bow. The* ENSEMBLE *disperses and suddenly an after-show party is underway. The young troupe members are having fun, fooling around with one another, drinking, singing, mingling with guests.*

Music is played by a little combo.

WIKTOR *and* IRENA *watch the celebrations, leaning against a large mirror.*

IRENA. I've had enough of this. Let's go.

WIKTOR. You go on. I'll follow you.

IRENA Let them have their fun. We can have our own.

An emotional KACZMAREK *joins them and leans against the mirror. He's a little tipsy.*

KACZMAREK. I'm off the hook! The Deputy Minister just told me! He loved it! Ha ha! Wants to meet us all in the morning! Talk about 'The Future'! I have to tell you something. I never believed in all this folky stuff. But this… tonight, this show, seeing it all come together, it moved me. You are a genius. To take something so… corny, right? Let's face it! This stuff is so corny! And make it so beautiful… Thank you, both. This is the most beautiful day of my life. Sing something, will you, Irena?

KACZMAREK *leads* IRENA *to the piano. She starts singing 'The Silent Child'.*

IRENA.
Sleep well, my silent child
The air outside is still
Till every debt is paid in full
No one should take you away…

WIKTOR *wanders downstage and he's…*

… outside on a balcony where ZULA *smokes. The sound of the song echoes behind them.*

ZULA (*looking in at* IRENA *singing*). So what is it between you two?

WIKTOR. Who?

ZULA. You and your sister.

WIKTOR (*takes her cigarette and drags on it*). Irena's not my sister.

ZULA. You're not brother and sister?

WIKTOR *just looks at her.* ZULA *takes his drink and knocks it back.*

No? Hansel and Gretel?

WIKTOR. No.

IRENA *sings a verse*.

IRENA.
Sleep now, my silent child
Sleep now, sleep now...

ZULA. She never makes you smile. When you're together.

WIKTOR. We're working.

ZULA (*scoffs*). Work?! This isn't work.

WIKTOR. No?

She looks at him.

ZULA. No. It's passion. (*She looks in his eyes*.) For me, anyhow. Doesn't music make you happy?

WIKTOR. Does it make you happy?

ZULA. I've been happy. I've been sad. She isn't making you happy. I can see that.

WIKTOR. Maybe she's not supposed to.

ZULA. Maybe someone else is.

WIKTOR. Who makes you happy? Anyone?

ZULA. Not yet.

IRENA *sings a verse*.

IRENA.
Sleep now, my silent child
Sleep now, unusual boy...

WIKTOR. So what's the story about your father?

ZULA looks at him, sceptically.

ZULA. Whose father?

WIKTOR Yours.

ZULA. What do you mean?

WIKTOR. I heard you got arrested. What happened?

ZULA. Are you interested in me because of my talent? Or just
   in general?

WIKTOR. In general.

ZULA. I see. He was drunk. He came into the wrong room,
   thought I was my mother, so I stabbed him with a knife
   I keep under my pillow.

   WIKTOR *looks alarmed.*

   He didn't die, don't worry.

WIKTOR. You always keep a knife under your pillow?

ZULA. You don't?

   WIKTOR *shakes his head.*

   So where is it?

   IRENA *finishes singing 'The Silent Child'.*

IRENA.
   Sleep now, my silent child
   Sleep now, unusual boy
   Sleep now, sleep now, sleep now

   WIKTOR *can't help himself. He moves towards* ZULA.
   *She looks into his eyes and takes his hand as the music swirls
   round them. Choral, orchestral… and it fades into a tinny
   transistorised sound, coming out of a little speaker on the
   desk of a government minister…*

   IRENA, WIKTOR *and* KACZMAREK *are attending an
   audience at the Ministry of Culture and Art. A portrait of the
   Polish president, Bolesław Bierut, and another of Joseph
   Stalin adorn the walls behind a high-ranking Party*
   DEPUTY MINISTER.

   IRENA *stares at* WIKTOR, *knowing everything is over
   between them, while the* MINISTER *taps his hand out of
   rhythm with the music…*

DEPUTY MINISTER. I can't help thinking about the war. When we couldn't sing our music. In your repertoire you access priceless, hidden treasures of our people's culture. This is highly commendable. We want you to become a living calling card for our fatherland.

IRENA. A calling card?

DEPUTY MINISTER. A cultural calling card.

IRENA. Like a postcard?

DEPUTY MINISTER. Yes! If you like. It's not like the old days now – where everything was a bloody stitch-up. This is a new broom and last night was a triumph. My wife was crying. She never cries. She's a very happy woman. But she's a closed woman – of average intelligence. And that's what made me think: this is power. What you're doing. It has power. Because it bypasses the brain – and cracks your heart open, right? And while we're in there – we can use it to say something.

IRENA. Say what?

DEPUTY MINISTER. Something about collective agricultural machinery. A strong number, with a good beat, hm? About land reform and the leader of the world proletariat. You know, happy, positive things. And we, in turn, will do everything in our power to show our gratitude. Make sure you're adequately resourced, I mean really, very… adequately. And then, who knows… Prague, Budapest, Moscow – Berlin! What do you think?

IRENA *clears her throat to speak. Everyone looks at her.*

IRENA. I would like to express gratitude on behalf of the ensemble for your appreciation. But when it comes to our repertoire, the whole intention is that it's based on authentic folk art.

WIKTOR *stares hard at* IRENA, *who is about to commit political suicide.*

DEPUTY MINISTER. Authentic what-what?

IRENA. Folk art. I grew up with these songs. I learnt them
    when I was a child. And I loved them – because as you say
    I didn't need to understand them. I already understood them.
    They're basic. They're about love, and death, and longing.
    The Germans came – we sang them. The Russians came…

KACZMAREK.…Liberated us…

IRENA. I mean liberated us – we sang them. It's all we had!
    Believe me, the rural population doesn't sing about the
    technicalities of economics.

DEPUTY MINISTER. Yes, yes, but I'm talking about things
    that are happening now. Land redistribution, cooperative
    factories. Exciting developments happening right now!

IRENA. Rural folk singers have never sung about land reform
    or this leader or that leader. They just don't do it. So it would
    be extremely difficult. So…

DEPUTY MINISTER (*sings*).
    'The devil knocked three times…'

    That particular song. It's not… not one of ours, is it?

IRENA. You don't like it?

DEPUTY MINISTER. It's not a question of liking it. It's a
    question of ethnic purity. I mean, isn't that what we're…?

IRENA. It's, well it's…

DEPUTY MINISTER. It was my wife pointed it out to me. It's
    Lemko, not Polish. Who authorised its use?

    KACZMAREK *looks at* IRENA.

IRENA. Well, we rearranged it, with entirely different lyrics,
    it's really its *musical* interest as far as we're…

DEPUTY MINISTER. But who brought it into the repertoire?

KACZMAREK (*looks at* WIKTOR). I think one of our younger
    singers… in a casual, moment of… I mean, entirely in
    ignorance, I imagine.

DEPUTY MINISTER. But *we* are not ignorant.

KACZMAREK. No. We are not.

DEPUTY MINISTER. The last thing we want is to inspire insurrectionists, is it not?

KACZMAREK. Is it n... It is not.

DEPUTY MINISTER. So who authorised it? It's a simple question.

IRENA. It's a... it's a folk song. We all... We amended the lyrics, and changed the... we, we didn't think it was... I authorised it because, as I say, musically...

DEPUTY MINISTER. I'm sorry, my dear, what is your name?

IRENA. Me?

DEPUTY MINISTER. Yes please.

IRENA. Irena Komorowska.

DEPUTY MINISTER (*writing*). Komor...

IRENA. Komorowska.

DEPUTY MINISTER. Thank you. (*Smiles.*) That's all I was asking. All right. Well, thank you all for coming today. As I say we really enjoyed last night. Interesting experiment. And good luck to you all and... thank you.

Everyone gets up to leave. KACZMAREK *shoots* IRENA *a desperate look and makes a bid for survival.*

KACZMAREK. If I may... my esteemed comrade's academic background is in history not politics. Her taste leans towards the undiluted, and perhaps slightly uneducated, older works from the ancient times of history rather than the bolder, more striking developments of today. Me? Look, I'm just an administrative manager. I am no artist like my comrades here, but I do believe, Comrade Bielecki, I believe to the depths of my soul, that our nation is no longer so ignorant as it once was in the past. I mean including its rural elements. Quite the contrary. As long as it is encouraged... and given direction as to what might *best* further the interests of our nation. This, I believe, is exactly what the role of our ensemble should be – to say… things. Thank you.

IRENA *turns to* WIKTOR, *looking for back-up. He looks down, avoiding her gaze.*

DEPUTY MINISTER. Well this is wonderful. We are all agreed! Please come through and join me for some lunch. We've laid out something for everyone.

KACZMAREK. Of course!

KACZMAREK *follows the* MINISTER.

DEPUTY MINISTER. Through here in the portrait room. Cigarette?

KACZMAREK. Of course! Thank you.

WIKTOR *waits for* IRENA. *She doesn't move.*

WIKTOR. Irena. Come on – we can eat.

IRENA *starts putting her stuff in her bag.*

Irena.

IRENA. Let's get out of here.

WIKTOR. I'm hungry.

IRENA. I'll buy you some dinner. Wiktor, you don't want to write songs about factories and combine harvesters.

WIKTOR. What are we supposed to do? At least we're on the inside here.

IRENA. Inside what?

WIKTOR *sighs.*

The only thing that's interesting about any of this – to me – is watching you, and realising you just never got the right bid till now.

WIKTOR. You're better than all the rest of us then.

IRENA. Who knows? Maybe I am! And at the risk of seeming conceited – the music *I* like? It's going to last longer than all that factory reform shit – 'cause as soon this whole charade falls apart no one's ever gonna sing any of it ever again. Are you coming with me?

WIKTOR *shakes his head.*

It's that girl, isn't it?

WIKTOR *looks down.*

(*Smiling sadly.*) And you know, I knew the second she walked in the door?

WIKTOR. I'm sorry.

IRENA *starts to leave but turns to him.*

IRENA. Did you ever love me?

WIKTOR. I must have.

IRENA. Good luck, Wiktor.

IRENA *goes.*

WIKTOR *comes downstage and turns his back to us. The* CHOIR *file on. The young singers and dancers are now all dressed in the green shirts and red scarves and ties of the ZMP.*

WIKTOR *conducts them in a huge hall. They sing a cantata about Stalin in front of a large audience. A giant poster of Stalin is hoisted up behind them.*

ENSEMBLE (*singing*).
Oh mountains from on high the eagle flies
We will ascend our mountain tops
With sunlight in our eyes.
Comrade Stalin's will is with us
New factories make machines
Fields lie down at our feet
Our land is modernised
Comrade Stalin!

Then they suddenly begin to recite an oath.

We swear to you, our fatherland, on the testament of the great patriots and revolutionaries, Felix Dzerzhinsky and Karol Świerczewski, to devote all our strength to the sacred cause of defending the peace against American and Nazi warmongers and perpetrators of genocide... And build everlasting friendship with the mighty Land of Soviets, the fatherland of Lenin and Stalin...

ZULA *sits on top of* WIKTOR, *who lies on the ground. She has his arms pinned to the floor.*

ZULA. I, Wiktor Zatoński, take you, Zuzanna Lichoń, to be my wife.

WIKTOR. I, Wiktor Zatoński tell you, Zuzanna Lichoń, to get off me.

ZULA. And I swear to be with you always, until death do us part.

WIKTOR. And I swear I'll brain you if you don't let me up.

ZULA. No, I swear to be with you always until death do us part. So help us God.

WIKTOR. Zula, there's a nail sticking in my arse. Right into a chilblain.

ZULA. It's what you deserve! I'll get up if you say it.

WIKTOR. Say what?

ZULA. Don't make me say it.

WIKTOR. What...

ZULA. You know.

WIKTOR. No. What?

ZULA. You know!

WIKTOR. What?

ZULA. Don't make me say it!

WIKTOR. Say what?

ZULA. I'm not saying it!

WIKTOR. Just say it. Say what you want me to say!

ZULA. No! If you ever say it, I'll say it. But I'm not ever gonna say it first.

WIKTOR. All right.

ZULA. You're not gonna say it?

WIKTOR. No. I'm good. I'll wait for you. And I'm very, very patient.

ZULA. I hate you! There – I said it.

ZULA grabs her sweater, pulling it on.

I can't stand this fucking place.

She gets up, stamping away the cold.

What you keep coming here for?

She scratches at a rash on her neck.

Look at this! That's poison ivy.

WIKTOR. That's not poison ivy, that's lice.

ZULA. Well they're your lice! I never had lice before.

WIKTOR. Well neither did I so… [*they must be yours.*] I like it here. That was actually a very good piano – before all the shrapnel.

ZULA. You seen? All those cots upstairs? Gives me the creeps. What are you working on out here anyway? In secret. Something for me?

WIKTOR. You?

ZULA. Kaczmarek says I'm the face of the orchestra.

WIKTOR. Excuse me?!

ZULA. Did you know we're going to Berlin?

WIKTOR. Really?

ZULA. The minister told me. Kaczmarek introduced me to him after our show. He wants us to tour all the great cities. Let me sing it.

WIKTOR. No, it's not for the show.

ZULA. Then I have to report it.

WIKTOR (*dubiously*). To who?

ZULA. Who do you think? Non-Soviet music is decadent. We all have to go to Kaczmarek every week to confess.

WIKTOR. Who does?

ZULA. All of us!

WIKTOR. Confess what?

ZULA. Don't look at me like that! You told them about Irena.

WIKTOR. What about her?

ZULA. That she was passing secrets.

WIKTOR. To who?

ZULA. I don't know! They're secrets! You told them.

WIKTOR. Who said that?

ZULA. Everyone says you ratted her out. They took her away.

WIKTOR. Were you followed here?

ZULA. No.

WIKTOR. What have you told them?

She looks at him.

About me.

ZULA. I never tell them anything.

WIKTOR. What don't you tell them?

ZULA. Honestly nothing. Don't get anxious. I just tell him stupid things – nothing. The worst part is, he thinks I fancy him. Can you imagine?

WIKTOR. What things?

ZULA. What?

WIKTOR. What do you tell him?

ZULA. The usual stuff! Nothing! He asked me if you're still in contact with Irena. I said I didn't know. He asked me if you have dollars stashed away somewhere. How would I know? What you did during the war...

WIKTOR. What do you say?

ZULA. What?

WIKTOR. About that.

ZULA. Nothing. Whatever makes him shut up and leave me alone. What would you do in my place? I'm on probation! They'll kick me out!

WIKTOR. Well done.

ZULA. All right, go and fuck yourself, bourgeois wanker.

ZULA *starts to go but turns back to him.*

If I wanted to – I could really fuck you up, you know. Kaczmarek says any little worm can betray someone they love, but it takes a real dickhead to betray his whole country!

WIKTOR. You don't know anything about me!

ZULA. Yes, that's becoming very clear. What difference does it make? I don't give a fuck about any of that stupid shit. You're all the fucking same! What?! What?! What do you want?!

WIKTOR *lets her go and turns away, spent and despondent. She stands helplessly.*

Silence. ZULA *goes to the piano and picks out a note or two, not really playing.* WIKTOR *watches her.*

WIKTOR. Remember when you said you could see me playing in places like Paris and New York.

ZULA. Mm.

WIKTOR. If that ever happened. Would you come with me?

ZULA. What would I do in Paris?

WIKTOR. You'd sing!

ZULA. I can't speak French.

WIKTOR You could learn. You have a good ear, I'd teach you.

ZULA. Really?

WIKTOR. Yes.

ZULA (*shrugs*). It's a nice dream.

WIKTOR. Maybe it's more than that.

ZULA. Then maybe you're mad.

WIKTOR. Maybe. Maybe everyone goes mad in this fucking shithole.

ZULA. I mean, how could I trust you anyway?

WIKTOR. You're asking *me* that?

It starts snowing as the ENSEMBLE *line up in the train station. They are singing* ZULA*'s song from* Jolly Fellows*: 'Foolish heart…'*

Everyone takes their places, sitting on long benches on the train, as they chug through the snowy countryside, trying to keep warm.

Lights flash past as KACZMAREK *walks up and down addressing the group.*

KACZMAREK. As you all know, these days Berlin is the front line between the socialist and the imperialist camp. And on the front line, as is the way with front lines, anything can happen. You'll meet all kinds of people with all kinds of stupid ideas. Maybe some of you already have. So we must stick together, be vigilant and responsible for one another. Whatever they say, Germans are still Germans. So here's to the adventure of a lifetime!

East Berlin, 1951.

Music erupts. The troupe whip off their coats to reveal their colourful costumes, and they launch into the climactic finale of their performance.

The ENSEMBLE *drift away to leave* ZULA *sitting alone at her table in the dressing room in the dark, lit only by the bulbs round her mirror.* WIKTOR *sits nearby.*

ZULA. That was amazing.

WIKTOR. Listen to me, Zula. This red line, that's where the Russian sector ends. It's four hundred metres from the stage door.

ZULA. Yes, I know. Yeah.

WIKTOR. Turn right out of stage door and keep going.

ZULA. I know. Yeah, yeah, okay.

WIKTOR. I'll wait for you there.

ZULA. I know.

KACZMAREK *brings some flowers to the table.*

KACZMAREK. What a triumph! Come on, Zula, join the celebrations! There are higher-ups here who want to meet you. What's the matter?

ZULA. Nothing. I had to fix my hair.

KACZMAREK. Wiktor, what are you doing? You coming in?

WIKTOR. No, I'm going to get an early night. Zula?

KACZMAREK. She's all right.

KACZMAREK *watches* WIKTOR *go.*

(*To* ZULA.) He only depresses everyone anyway. You look beautiful.

ZULA. Thank you. I'll follow you down.

KACZMAREK. It's all right. I'll wait. You know, here, in Berlin, you can just walk across to the west? There are no borders, nothing. People live in the east, work in the west, they go back and forth all day long. They don't know if they're coming or going. Our lot are always watching us of course.

I know what Wiktor is suggesting.

She looks at him.

It's all right. That you slip away, separately, tonight. That the west will welcome you with open arms. And then, that you could go anywhere. London, Paris. America, God forbid. I've told our lot to let him go. And you want my advice? You let him go too. Don't follow him. Enjoy the party. You and me? We're made of the same stuff. Wiktor? I don't think so. I won't get into it. I don't think I need to! You already feel it in your bones. I know you do. You belong with us, Zula. This is your destiny. You hear that crowd tonight? You're on the cusp of magnificence. Don't roll the dice. You'll be with me. It'll be all right.

ZULA *is dragged to the piano. The* PARTYGOERS *cry out for her to sing. There is silence for a moment and then she sings the first verse of 'What Is It I Need That I Don't Already Have?'*

ZULA.
What is it that I need that I don't already have?
Who was there in the past that I couldn't seem to save?
But will I seem so smart, me and my broken heart
When I am pretending to be brave?

A SOLDIER *comes and dances with* ZULA. ANIA *starts singing the next verse.* WIKTOR *stands to the side, putting on his coat. He watches* ZULA *for a moment, then slips away.*

ANIA.
What is there up ahead that I can't already see?
Startling as it seems, well, it's supposed to be
Where am I going next?
And if no one objects
Just close the door and that'll be the end of me

ANIA *and* PIANIST.

>But I'll never be contented, repent or ever be lamented
>Till I'm planted down like rotten crops
>And covered up with weeds

KACZMAREK.

>What is it that I want that I can't already taste?
>A damson from a tree
>A girl that I once chased
>A girl who ran away and wanted to be caught
>Then bade farewell to my love like some merchandise she
>>bought

ANIA sings the last verse as ZULA *dances close to the*
SOLDIER, held tightly in his arms.

ANIA.

>What is it that I need that I don't already have?
>Who was there in the past that I couldn't even see?
>But will I seem so smart, me and my broken heart
>When I am pretending to be free?
>When I am pretending to be free?
>When I am pretending to be free?

The SOLDIER *dancing with* ZULA *begins to dance the*
Madison...

Paris, 1955.

An old-fashioned film leader with numbers counting down
from ten to one... Light fades on ZULA.

In the foreground, bathed by the projection, WIKTOR
conducts a little band of MUSICIANS *playing the score for*
a film. Some DANCERS *rehearse the Madison for the movie...*

The rehearsal ends and a music producer, MICHEL, *leads*
two FILM PRODUCERS *in.*

MICHEL *(in French)*. Well done! Wiktor! Nice work, everybody!
These are finest musicians in Paris, you know, this is...
Wiktor – *(In English.)* might I introduce our producers of the
movie. This is Delia. This is Herbert. They flew in last night.

WIKTOR. Welcome. Thank you for coming.

DELIA. It's wonderful. *Trés hip*.

MICHEL. '*Super-cool.*'

HERBERT. You really bring out the moment, I mean this is... now.

DELIA. Yes...

WIKTOR. Well. I've only done the music. I didn't do the... Thank you for the opportunity.

HERBERT. No! Thank you! What key is this piece in?

WIKTOR. Eh, A minor.

HERBERT. A minor, A minor, I thought so. Yes, is that – you know the chord where they turn and it's da-da-daaah...

WIKTOR. Mm-hm.

HERBERT. You've got a diminished fifth in there under the... what's the bass playing...?

WIKTOR. Eh... B flat.

HERBERT. Right, because you go to C there, right? Da-da-daaah-da-da...

WIKTOR (*looking*). I don't...

HERBERT. Sorry, C sharp.

WIKTOR. E?

HERBERT. Right, E! That's what I... Because are you... If the bass went to E major there instead, right?

MICHEL. Absolutely, I love that.

HERBERT. Because then you get that tension, that dissonance – I mean it's just going to...

MICHEL. It'll kill everybody.

HERBERT. It'll kill 'em.

WIKTOR. Okay...

HERBERT. Because then instead of da-dadaaah. Which is fine, don't get me wrong, I mean that's fine, but if it's more... Da-da-daaah-daaah-daaahh you know they're *turning* you know, and it's like... Da-da-daaah-daaaahh!!

MICHEL. I love that.

DELIA. Let's try it.

MICHEL. Yeah, we'll – absolutely, right?

The MUSICIANS *are packing their stuff away.*

WIKTOR. It's – yes, just right now... (*Glances at the clock.*) The union rules – the musicians need to...

MICHEL. Yes! Le Syndicate! Union rules – the musicians have got to finish. Or you can pay, Herbert! I mean, I don't mind!

HERBERT. No that's fine, ha ha! Do it tomorrow! What is this piece anyhow? You compose it?

WIKTOR. Well, kind of... It's based on an old Eastern European...

DELIA. What's that accent?

MICHEL. Wiktor is from Poland.

DELIA. Oh like Chopin!

MICHEL. Exactly like Chopin!

HERBERT. You have zero trace of an accent.

DELIA. Zero.

MICHEL. Right? Listen, I'll see you outside, we'll let everyone...

HERBERT. Of course.

DELIA. You'll join us for a drink?

WIKTOR. Yes, of course.

MICHEL. Thanks, everyone – we're done for today.

(*To* WIKTOR.) Quick drink?

WIKTOR. Actually, I can't.

MICHEL. What are you talking about? It's not even midnight! Wiktor, this pair could be a lucrative new source of income. Your music actually makes this stupid scene work! They just want to take you for a glass of champagne at Lady Margaux.

WIKTOR. I promised Juliette I'd be home for dinner. It's her birthday.

MICHEL. Let me call her, I'll explain. Don't mess this up for us!

WIKTOR. Just tell her one drink.

WIKTOR *stands and picks up his coat. A woman,* AIMEE, *is putting her earrings in.* WIKTOR *is drinking.*

AIMEE. What do you keep coming here for?

WIKTOR. What do you care? I just want to sit here.

AIMEE. Maybe that's the problem. I feel a little insulted. No one else seems to get sadder the longer they're here. They usually go straight in the bedroom, but with you… You pay me to watch you drink? Don't tell me – I remind you of someone. But hey, it's your money. Or maybe you should go to her. At least your heartache won't cost you a fortune there.

WIKTOR (*gives a little laugh*). I can't.

AIMEE. Because she's with someone else?

WIKTOR. I've no idea. It's been years.

AIMEE. How do I remind you of her? How I look?

WIKTOR. No. Not really.

AIMEE. My body?

WIKTOR *shakes his head.*

So how? My voice? You like when I sing. I know you do.

WIKTOR *smiles, shrugs a little.*

(*Sings.*)
Do you love her?
Or is it still too soon to know?

WIKTOR *nods, shrugs*.

When I think back, a couple of days
Before I found you in her spell
Was there a warning?
What can I say? Should I look away?
It's still too soon to know.

Is that like her voice?

WIKTOR (*shrugs*). No, completely different. It's more how...
you see through me. So, I don't have to bother, you know...

AIMEE. What?

WIKTOR. Pretending.

AIMEE. Pretending what?

WIKTOR. That I belong.

AIMEE. In Paris?

WIKTOR. Anywhere.

AIMEE. Well, I'm sorry to disappoint you, but I don't actually
see through you. I don't see anything.

WIKTOR. Right. What's that music?

AIMEE. Where?

WIKTOR. Where is it? The street?

AIMEE. Probably from downstairs. He's an old drunk.

WIKTOR *starts to go*.

Hey.

WIKTOR. Hm?

AIMEE. Will you do me a favour?

WIKTOR. What?

AIMEE. Don't come back here.

WIKTOR *stands there as* AIMEE *leaves*.

WIKTOR *looks crumpled. It's late. His French lover,* JULIETTE, *comes to a desk and starts typing.* WIKTOR *throws his coat on a chair, goes to a bureau and pours himself a drink, looking out in the night.*

JULIETTE (*glancing up at him*). Have you been whoring?

WIKTOR. What?

JULIETTE. When you skulk in like that and don't say hello it usually means you've been whoring.

WIKTOR. I don't have money for whores.

JULIETTE. What a pity.

WIKTOR. I knew you were working. I didn't want to disturb you. Here, happy birthday. I'm sorry I'm late.

He hands her a present. She opens it. It's a book.

JULIETTE. *Collected Polish Folk Verse, third edition.*

She opens it and reads his inscription.

'For the woman of my dreams.'

She puts the book down.

Whoever that is…

WIKTOR. This is where you're supposed to say, 'And you're the man of mine.'

JULIETTE (*typing*). The man of my dreams has a yacht in San Tropez.

WIKTOR. Well, I may be on my way. Michel wants me to do music for another movie.

JULIETTE. Well, that's good!

WIKTOR. Mm. You get much done?

JULIETTE. Just notes for my talk.

WIKTOR *looks at her blankly.*

The talk I'm giving. In Amsterdam?

WIKTOR. Oh yes, when is it?

JULIETTE. Are you serious? Saturday! I've told you about eleven times. I'll be back on Monday. You won't even miss me.

WIKTOR. Of course I will.

JULIETTE (*unconvinced*). Mmm.

> WIKTOR *goes to the record player, puts on some music.* JULIETTE *comes to him. He holds her. They listen to the music for a moment.*

I'd love for us to write something together. Wouldn't it be fun?

WIKTOR. I tried something with your poem.

JULIETTE. Which one?

WIKTOR. 'The Pendulum.'

JULIETTE. Will you play it for me?

WIKTOR. I didn't compose new music for it, I just kind of set it to…

JULIETTE. An old Polish folk tune.

WIKTOR. It was rearranged, I mean, you'd hardly know, but… it… yes. It kind of works.

JULIETTE. Polish folk tunes! We should write something modern. Original! Something that's – you know, really ours, together.

WIKTOR. No, arranging's where it's at for me right now. Whatever I write it's always too…

JULIETTE. What…

WIKTOR. Convoluted. Michel says popular songs need a kind of simplicity so that anyone can understand them. They can't be too philosophical.

JULIETTE. Depends who you're writing for. I don't feel like talking down to anybody.

She goes towards the kitchenette.

Let's eat this dinner, I always find it very interesting to eat at three a.m. Too late for dinner, too early for breakfast. (*Off.*) There's a letter for you.

WIKTOR. Where?

JULIETTE (*off*). On my desk.

WIKTOR *picks up the letter, but seeing the handwriting he suddenly doesn't want to open it.*

Just then, ZULA *comes into the apartment. She looks like she is waiting for somebody.*

What is it?

WIKTOR. Probably nothing.

JULIETTE *comes back, placing a pot on a trivet on the table.* WIKTOR *watches as* ZULA *sits down near the window.*

JULIETTE. Just let me wash my hands and we can eat. Wiktor?

WIKTOR (*staring at* ZULA). Yes?

JULIETTE (*playfully looking at him*). You know I love you.

WIKTOR. I love you.

JULIETTE *goes.*

WIKTOR *smiles faintly. The light changes as he approaches* ZULA. *She looks different somehow – more elegant and mature. The old record continues to play... but now it's on the jukebox in a little café bar.*

ZULA *sees* WIKTOR. *She stands.*

ZULA. Is this all right?

WIKTOR. Yes, no I like it here. I've been here before.

He joins her and they sit. Neither knows what to say for a moment. A WAITER *brings a bottle and some glasses.*

Sorry, can I get a... just some vodka, thank you. How long have you been in Paris?

ZULA. Since yesterday. I leave tomorrow.

WIKTOR. You look well.

ZULA. Don't lie.

WIKTOR. I didn't read anything about the troupe performing here.

ZULA. I'm not here with the troupe.

WIKTOR. You left?

ZULA. No, but I can travel legally now, so...

WIKTOR. How so?

ZULA. I have Italian citizenship!

WIKTOR. What?!

ZULA. I married a Sicilian. Mm. And gained Italian citizenship.

WIKTOR. That's... that's wonderful.

ZULA. So I could come and find you.

She laughs. WIKTOR *laughs uncertainly.*

Are you with someone? Am I too late?

WIKTOR. Yes. Are you?

ZULA. I'm married.

WIKTOR. Oh yes.

ZULA. You already forgot?

The WAITER *brings a glass of vodka for* WIKTOR.

WIKTOR. No, I'm... just when you said it was so you could find me. For a second I didn't realise you were...

ZULA. Married?

WIKTOR. ....Joking.

ZULA. Mm.

Silence.

(*Suddenly.*) You drink now.

WIKTOR. It's different here.

ZULA. So tell me… tell me everything.

WIKTOR. Well. I work.

ZULA. Playing music.

WIKTOR. Mm-hm. Arranging, composing. I back singers at a club. I'm doing the score for a film.

ZULA. Oh!

WIKTOR. It's good. I don't quite understand it – the story I mean, but… it's… People might like it.

ZULA. You don't understand it because – what – it isn't clear what it's about or because you're still stupid, or…?

WIKTOR. I don't know. I'm not sure the film-makers understand what it's about either! It's a French film.

They smile.

Are you happy?

ZULA *smiles and shrugs.*

Happily married, I mean.

ZULA *smiles.*

Where did you meet your husband?

ZULA. In Prague. He's an electrical engineer. He saw me performing. He sent me flowers.

WIKTOR. Romantic.

ZULA. Not really.

WIKTOR. So where is home now?

ZULA. Palermo.

WIKTOR. Palermo? Mm. What's it like?

ZULA. It's warm. A little bit lonely. (*She smiles*.)

WIKTOR. But you still… you still perform with the troupe?

ZULA. My husband doesn't mind. He knows it's important.

WIKTOR. No, but I mean, they let you… I mean…

ZULA. Yes, it's important. It's cultural… I don't do it as much as I… you know. But they trust me. And Kaczmarek is quite well respected these days now. He's…

WIKTOR. Of course he is.

ZULA. He makes things happen.

WIKTOR. I can imagine. Can I ask… what happened? Why you didn't…?

ZULA (*nods, shrugs*). I suddenly felt like I wasn't good enough.

WIKTOR. Good enough how?

ZULA. Good as you. In general.

WIKTOR. So what do you… Why have you… what's happening?

ZULA. I don't know. I can't say. I mean, I came because it's… it's either very simple or terribly complicated.

Her face crumples. She sits in silence.

WIKTOR. So… what do you want to do?

ZULA. Find out?

The WAITER *comes with the bill.*

WAITER. We're closing, you can settle up at the bar.

WIKTOR. Can we get one more?

WAITER. It's the boss – I can't. Chez Marlette stays open, you could go there.

ZULA *wipes her face with a napkin. The* WAITER *leaves.*

ZULA. Sorry.

WIKTOR (*shakes his head*). So what's your name now?

ZULA. Gangarossa-Lichoń.

WIKTOR Ganga... what?

ZULA. Gangarossa. It's Sicilian.

They laugh.

It wasn't a church wedding, so it doesn't count. You're not married... Are you?

WIKTOR. I think I've been waiting for you.

The BAND *takes over the song from the jukebox and plays.* AIMEE *is singing 'Still Too Soon to Know'.*

AIMEE.
Are you sorry? Or is it still too soon to know?
It didn't take much to break us in two
For it was in the way that she came close to touching you
The look in your eyes
I thought I recognised
It's still too soon to know

It's late. WIKTOR *and* ZULA *have been drinking all night.*
They fall about dancing in each other's arms.

And it's still too soon to know
Will you stay or will you go?
It's still too soon to know

The BAND *reach a crescendo. Then quieten to...*

When I think back, a couple of days
If I wasn't happy then
I never will be
I wonder was this
Ignorance or bliss
It's still too soon...

Blackout.

ACT TWO

Paris, 1957.

WIKTOR *joins the* BAND *at the piano while* ZULA *is in a stunning black dress.*

ZULA *sings, a jazz rendition of 'I Do' with* WIKTOR*'s band. The audience sit at little tables amidst cigarette smoke and bustling* WAITERS.

ZULA *finishes to enthusiastic applause.* WIKTOR *looks at her from his spot at the piano, admiring her effect on the audience. She turns around to look at him.*

ZULA *and* WIKTOR *are in their attic flat.* ZULA *lies in* WIKTOR*'s lap, reading through some lyrics…*

ZULA (*sings*).
'Figure hanging on a leather band
Cog consults the watch he cups in his hand'

It doesn't fit the music.

WIKTOR. It fits when you pronounce it properly.

ZULA. And it doesn't make sense. Isn't a cog actually inside a watch?

WIKTOR. Mm-hm.

ZULA. So how can the cog be 'consulting' the watch? The cog is *inside* the watch. 'Bejewelled movement measures lost and vanished time…' What the hell does it even mean? And this bit later on 'The pendulum killed time…'

WIKTOR. No.

ZULA. Is this actually translated from Polish?

WIKTOR Yes, but it's more of a… free translation.

ZULA. There's free and there's running rampant. Who translated it? Juliette? Your poetess?

WIKTOR Yes. So what? She did it as a favour. For nothing.

ZULA. I should hope so. 'The pendulum killed time.' Oh my god!

WIKTOR. Say what you like. Juliette is very well known in Paris. They just brought out her anthology.

ZULA. Oh! (*Gently mocking imitation of him.*) 'They just brought out her anthology', did they? 'Her anthology.' Well, I won't be singing that.

WIKTOR. Then there'll be no record.

ZULA. Then there won't be. Oi! By the way – when did you ask her to do this?

WIKTOR. Last week.

ZULA. Last week?! She works too fast. You never said you were meeting her.

WIKTOR. I didn't meet her. I bumped into her.

ZULA. You didn't tell me you bumped into her. She still angry with you?

WIKTOR. She was never angry with me.

ZULA. No?

WIKTOR. This isn't Poland, Zula. People don't throw themselves in the nearest river every time someone breaks up. It's just life here. It's just natural.

ZULA. Is that what you're like too?

WIKTOR. You don't need to be jealous.

ZULA. Why would I be jealous?

WIKTOR. You got married – not me. Are you ready?

ZULA. No. I need a drink.

WIKTOR. Everything's all right, Zula! The only thing you need to remember is just be nice to Michel, he can be helpful.

WIKTOR *is doing up his tie*.

We like each other, and he likes you even more.

ZULA. Is that why he's always staring at me?

WIKTOR. No.

ZULA. Then why?

WIKTOR. Because you're charming. But go easy on the make-up.

ZULA. Why?

WIKTOR. You look good already. Michel is always banging on about women who wear too much make-up. It's one of his... Just be yourself. Relax. No one wants to change anything about you. But...

ZULA. What?

WIKTOR. Nothing. Just Michel likes you. If he knows you like him too... it's just...

ZULA. It's what?

WIKTOR. It's nice. For everybody.

ZULA. It's nice?

WIKTOR. Yes, be nice. That's all.

She touches WIKTOR.

ZULA. Like this? Or this? You tell me, how nice do you want me to be to him?

WIKTOR. I don't know, you decide. Tie or no tie?

ZULA. Tie.

WIKTOR *removes his tie*.

While we're on the subject. Will Juliette be there tonight?

WIKTOR. Probably yes. Zula – she's already had two lovers since me.

ZULA. But who's counting, right?

WIKTOR. Are you ready?

ZULA. Wiktor?

WIKTOR. What? It's almost nine o' clock.

ZULA. I don't care.

> *She goes to him. They embrace passionately. They are*
> *engulfed by* BOHEMIAN PARTYGOERS, *some dancing to*
> *music, some laughing and drinking. Someone plays the*
> *double bass. It's a trendy avant-garde scene. Some people at*
> *the party start to line-dance, like the 'Madison' dance scene*
> *in Jean-Luc Godard's* Bande à part. ZULA *arrives with*
> WIKTOR. *She immediately copies the dance, joining in,*
> *picking it up quickly.*

MICHEL. Wiktor! And Zula! Finally.

WIKTOR. Michel. You know Zula.

MICHEL. Of course! And I'm often slipping in down the back –
to wa… to hear you singing at the club. Wow.

ZULA. Thank you.

WIKTOR. How's the new cut of the film?

MICHEL. The investors are very happy. Which is good news
for you too, of course. We got into Cannes! We should all go.
You should hear what Wiktor's done.

WIKTOR. It's just some rearranged old pieces.

MICHEL. That music wasn't original?

WIKTOR. No. But traditional, out of copyright.

MICHEL. Thank God!

ZULA. Wiktor is fantastic at going over old ground for new
potatoes.

MICHEL. Well, I love that. And I love the whole 'out of
copyright' notion! We should do an album – just that stuff.
But redone, you know, for now, the way you do it, now.

WIKTOR. You think?

ZULA. You converse away, I'll look around.

ZULA walks off. MICHEL *watches her as she goes.*

MICHEL. She's really got something, hasn't she?

WIKTOR. What?

MICHEL. You know. Something. She has something!

ZULA moves through the apartment and picks up two martinis from a passing tray. She dances for a few moments. Drinks one drink, discards the glass, and walks right up to JULIETTE, who's busy conversing with some guests in a quiet corner.

ZULA. Good evening.

JULIETTE (*to her friends*). Excuse me.

JULIETTE turns to face ZULA.

ZULA. I've thought a lot about your lyrics.

JULIETTE. Really? What lyrics?

ZULA. For that song Wiktor asked you to do.

JULIETTE. Oh yes.

ZULA. 'The pendulum has killed time.' Nice, but I didn't get it.

JULIETTE. You don't what?

ZULA. I didn't get it. I don't understand it!

JULIETTE. Oh that's all right! It's just a metaphor.

ZULA. A metaphor for what?

JULIETTE. That time doesn't matter when you're in love.

JULIETTE forces a tight little smile.

ZULA. But that's not true though, is it? Time means everything when you're in love.

JULIETTE. Sorry, what?

ZULA. Time means everything when you're in love.

JULIETTE. Oh. Okay.

ZULA. What is it? My accent?

JULIETTE. No, I just couldn't... Well look, I suppose it just depends on what you mean by time then, doesn't it? Time together. Time apart.

ZULA. I don't know. I don't think so. But anyway, here's the problem. Are you listening?

JULIETTE. Yes.

ZULA. The pendulum doesn't kill time. It marks time.

JULIETTE. It's a metaphor. It's not a literal thing. It doesn't have to mean the same thing for everybody. (*She laughs.*) I mean I can't stand here discussing the nature of... time! Philosophers have struggled with that one for aeons!

ZULA. For what?

JULIETTE. For aeons!

ZULA. Oh for aeons? Well, regardless, what can I say? I can't sing something that makes no sense. It will just have to be redone for the record.

JULIETTE. Sounds like you should do it yourself.

ZULA. I'll have to.

JULIETTE. Or get Wiktor to change it for you.

ZULA. He doesn't do original work.

JULIETTE. Oh yes.

ZULA. So.

JULIETTE. Do you like it here?

ZULA. What? In this flat?

JULIETTE. No, I mean Paris.

ZULA. Paris? It's okay.

JULIETTE. It must have been a shock.

ZULA. Why a shock?

JULIETTE. I don't know. All the cinemas, cafés, restaurants, shops.

ZULA. Toilets?

JULIETTE. No, I mean compared to... I mean, I'm only talking about as far as I know...

ZULA. Between you and me, my life was better in Poland.

JULIETTE. So why did you run away?

ZULA. I didn't run away. I married an Italian and emigrated legally.

JULIETTE. Right.

ZULA. Ever been to Palermo? In Sicily?

JULIETTE. Sicily? No.

ZULA. That's a shame. You should travel. Paris is nice but it's not, you know... It's a big world.

JULIETTE. It's a big what?

ZULA. World! It's a big world. You know, world?

JULIETTE. I know.

> ZULA *raises her martini glass.*

ZULA. Nice meeting you. We should be friends.

JULIETTE. Yes, I'd like that.

ZULA. I like your aeons.

JULIETTE. What?

ZULA. Your earrings. And your shoes.

JULIETTE. Thank you. I like yours too.

ZULA. Thank you.

WIKTOR *has been prevailed upon to play the piano.*
MICHEL *dances with* ZULA, *talking intimately.* MICHEL
has had a few drinks and is clearly animated chatting with her.

ZULA *breaks away and marches over to* WIKTOR, *furious,
drunkenly accosting him, while* MICHEL *dances with
others, oblivious.*

Excuse me. Can I have a word with you?

WIKTOR (*drunk*). Not now! Come on, everybody's going to
The Eclipse.

WIKTOR *grabs* ZULA*'s coat, holding it for her to put on.*

ZULA. I met your lover by the way.

The PARTYGOERS *spill out of the flat, heading to a club.*

And I had a very interesting conversation with your new
patron, Michel.

WIKTOR. Good! It's good that he likes you.

Traffic swells around them, night city noise, as WIKTOR
leads ZULA *into the street.*

ZULA. What the fuck did you tell him?

WIKTOR What?

ZULA. Michel. What did you tell Michel about me?

WIKTOR. Nothing! Very little.

ZULA. Oh very little, just that I'm a liar. I pretended to be
a village girl to get in your programme. That I was on
probation – for *killing* my father?

WIKTOR. Yes, well, maybe that was...

ZULA. That I danced for Stalin at the Kremlin.

WIKTOR. Come on. That was a nice touch.

ZULA. Why would you say that?

WIKTOR. Michel was looking for something journalists might
like. It's not important. They call it colour.

ZULA. Colour?!

They are handing in their coats at a cloakroom in the jazz club, music swelling.

WIKTOR. That's how it works here. Michel is paying for a recording session. He needs to be able to sell it so he can get a return on his investment. It's not a big deal. Nobody minds anything you did – as long as it's interesting. Edith Piaf worked in a brothel, and they love her all the more for it.

ZULA. A brothel! What the hell are you doing to me?! And my ex-husband isn't an Italian duke, he makes spark plugs in a factory.

WIKTOR. Christ, all right, I won't do it again. Let's just go home.

ZULA. No, I'm going to the club.

Music swells as they enter the club. The crowd from the party are buzzing, enjoying the band.

(*Shouting over the din.*) I met your lover by the way. Did I tell you that? Nice. I suppose you could say she's pretty if she wasn't a bit on the old side. But what can she do about that? Nothing. There's nothing she can do. Because of all the bloody aeons flying by. Oh well. You look good together.

WIKTOR. Zula…

ZULA turns on her heel, grabbing a bottle of brandy off a table on the way. She sits with some men.

ZULA. 'It's a metaphor,' she says. What an idiot!

She takes a swig. Suddenly, Bill Haley's 'Rock Around the Clock' starts to play. The party livens up. ZULA gets up, head bouncing to the rhythm. She dances across the room, dancing with different men, changing partners, loving the song.

ZULA climbs up on a bar. WIKTOR comes to get her down. She shakes her skirt at him, like a matador to a bull.

She loses her balance – opens her arms wide – and jumps from the bar, caught in the nick of time by some PARTYGOERS.

The music and nightlife melt away as WIKTOR *carries* ZULA *into the apartment. They lie down.* ZULA *climbs on top of* WIKTOR.

Repeat after me... I, Wiktor Zatoński take you, Zuzanna Lichoń, to be my wife. Go on. No? And I swear to be with you always, until death do us part. No?

WIKTOR *lies there insensibly.*

Because I, Zuzanna Lichoń, take you, Wiktor Zatoński, to be my husband. And I swear to be with you always until death do us part. So help us God. So help us... You were different in Poland. You were a man... there.

She falls asleep. Music plays. WIKTOR *goes to the piano, the lights change...*

Paris, 1958.

...WIKTOR *is working out a tune.* ZULA *comes, eating a bowl of breakfast.*

What is that?

WIKTOR. Michel says we need a duet. For your album.

ZULA. With who?

WIKTOR. He's talking to some singers.

ZULA. Women? Men?

WIKTOR. Men.

ZULA. A duet for me and some man? 'Pid' in French?

WIKTOR. Of course.

ZULA. It's so cheesy like that!

WIKTOR. Let me work on it. Michel reckons it could be a hit.

ZULA. Maybe like some kind of novelty hit! What I want to know is what happened to all the other things we were working on.

WIKTOR. No, Michel loves the whole... you know, reworking old Polish songs into...

ZULA. Cheesy pop?

WIKTOR. It's more jazz surely.

ZULA. If you say so.

WIKTOR. And if it goes well and they trust us, you know, that
we're…

ZULA. Desperate.

WIKTOR. Amenable. Someone they can work with. Then on
the next one we can…

ZULA. You know what would be nice as a duet? The one you
were working on before with Juliette. Her pendulum song.

WIKTOR (*dubiously*). Mm. You like that one now?

ZULA (*coming to piano to find it*). Well, no, not… Well yes,
I mean it's actually… 'cause it's about time and… it's… I've
changed a few things, got rid of the pendulum line – only to
make everything fit but… Your music is gorgeous. I mean
it's…

WIKTOR. I already know what Michel will say.

ZULA. Who cares?

WIKTOR. The whole concept is Polish folk songs reworked
for…

ZULA. For who?

WIKTOR. For now. I really need to finish this.

ZULA. Three minutes of your life.

  ZULA *sings 'The Favourite Hour'.*

  Figure hanging on a leather band
  Cog consults the watch he cups in his hand
  Bejewelled movement measures lost and vanished time
  Pray for the boy who makes his bed in cold earth and
    quicklime

  So stay the hands, arrest the time
  Till I am captured by your touch

Blessings I don't count, small mercies and such
The flags may lower as we approach the favourite hour

Put out my eyes so I may never spy
Waving branches as they're waving goodbye
Their vile perfume brings to my mouth a bitter taste
The murmuring brooks had best speak up, it's a terrible
    waste…

So stay the hands, arrest the time
Till I am captured by your touch
Blessings I don't count, small mercies and such
The flags may lower as we approach the favourite hour

As she finishes, WIKTOR *doesn't really react.*

No?

She goes and picks up her breakfast.

WIKTOR (*tries to improve the mood*). I didn't hear you come in
last night.

ZULA. You were snoring, I slept on the sofa.

WIKTOR. Where were you?

ZULA. That little Polish bar on Île Saint-Louis.

WIKTOR. Again?

ZULA. They speak Polish! I like it. I can relax. No one
understands my accent here. It's exhausting. You never think
of going home? Just for a rest?

WIKTOR (*laughs*). A rest? I'd be breaking rocks in a quarry for
twenty years. (*Shakes his head.*) There's no one there – for
me, any more.

ZULA. I'd be there.

WIKTOR. Right.

ZULA. When we were small, when the wind whistled through
the windows in our apartment, at night. My sister Alicja used
to say that it was God singing.

WIKTOR. You know I can't go back.

ZULA. No, I know that. I just wondered if you ever feel, you know, that you ever felt like you ever... wanted to, that's all. Anyway why are you asking me where I was? You're never here.

WIKTOR. When?

ZULA. All the time.

WIKTOR. No I'm not.

ZULA. I'd come with you, you know. Anywhere you want to go.

WIKTOR. I don't actually go anywhere. I just sometimes need to walk.

ZULA. I need to walk too. You mean alone.

WIKTOR. It's just how I hear things, get ideas. Is it a problem?

ZULA. Not necessarily. Of course not. I just sometimes wonder what I'm doing here. That's all. I didn't mean to stop you working. Go on.

She puts her breakfast away.

WIKTOR *is playing the track for the duet.* ZULA *puts headphones on, coming to a microphone. A* MALE SINGER *steps to the microphone. Two* FEMALE BACKING SINGERS *are doing 'Oooohs...' They are in a recording studio. A red light comes on to indicate the tape is rolling.*

The MALE SINGER *sings a jazzy version of 'Pid Oblaczkom' into a big microphone.*

When it's ZULA*'s turn, she sings in a flat monotone.*

WIKTOR. Stop!

ZULA. What?

WIKTOR What are you doing?

ZULA. Singing.

The red light blinks off.

WIKTOR (*coming to* ZULA).What happened to what we rehearsed?

ZULA. Just let me sing it. I'm not sure I like what we rehearsed. Now that I hear him singing.

WIKTOR. But that's just dead.

ZULA. Dead?

WIKTOR. Put something into it, for Christ's sake.

ZULA. Like what?

WIKTOR. Like what we rehearsed.

ZULA. I'm just matching his energy.

WIKTOR. That's his style – you're different. If you turned on the radio and you heard this dead voice coming out would you want to go and buy that record?

ZULA. No, I'd feel sorry for the girl.

WIKTOR. What are you sorry about?

ZULA. Listen to the song. She ran into the woods – and there was nothing there.

WIKTOR. Well put something there. We have forty minutes left.

ZULA. What about if… hold on.

She takes off her headphones and comes to the piano. She plays and sings along.

When I sing, if you change key here to… (*She plays.*) or no wait. If it changes to – (*She plays.*) it opens it up, and it's not so…

WIKTOR (*angrily*). We don't have time for this.

MICHEL*'s voice comes over the talkback speaker.*

MICHEL (*off*). Wiktor? All good? Zula? It's sounding good!

Pause – ZULA doesn't respond.

You want a break?

ZULA *goes back to the microphone.* ZULA *and* WIKTOR
are silent.

We have time. It's sounding good. Let's try another take.
We'll roll again.

ZULA. It's fine. I'll do it. You'll get what you want.

WIKTOR. Don't do it just for me. Everything here is for you.

ZULA. For me – not you?

WIKTOR. Yes. Don't worry, it sounds good. Believe in yourself.

ZULA. I do. It's you I don't believe in.

WIKTOR. Okay.

MICHEL (*off; voice coming over the talkback*). Okay. Wiktor?
Okay?

WIKTOR. Apologies, everybody, just a misunderstanding. Let's
go again.

MICHEL. Rolling.

The red light comes on. ZULA *starts again.* WIKTOR
*conducts the band. The song bleeds into a recording on
a gramophone.*

Paris, 1959.

KACZMAREK *is standing in* WIKTOR *and* ZULA's
*apartment, listening to their album, reading the sleeve,
turning it over and over, reading it, listening to it.*

KACZMAREK. It's so strange. I recognise all of these – but it's
like I'm hearing them for the first time.

WIKTOR. Brings them to a new audience.

KACZMAREK. Yes! A new market.

WIKTOR. Our producer, Michel, says if the company had spent
a little more on advertising it could have gone in the charts.

KACZMAREK. They should have! Can't they do it now? Give
it another push?

WIKTOR. I think it's probably had its chance... But maybe if we try another one.

ZULA. If they'll pay for another one.

KACZMAREK. No, they should! It wouldn't surprise me if they do. In point of fact, you wouldn't believe some of the changes back home, you know. I'm sort of what people here would call a... well, a promoter now. Not just for our old orchestra. Lots of acts. Tours, concerts, Zula. Little trips like this now too. This is my third time in Paris. I was in Rome last year. I've no one as good as you though, Zula. We miss you. You too of course, Wiktor. Life is so unpredictable really, isn't it? Can I buy this?

WIKTOR. No! Keep it.

KACZMAREK. Thank you, it's... Blimey! How about you, Zula? You like it here? You like Paris?

ZULA. Yes of course. It's great. But it's different. At home everybody knows where they stand, don't they?

KACZMAREK. Yes, we do...

ZULA. You know what you have to do, how to hustle your way along...

KACZMAREK. ...Everybody knows the game... who the good guys are – who the bastards are.

ZULA. ...But here, it's like everything is up for grabs...

KACZMAREK. ...You've got to be up early. I'm a bit of a bastard myself...

ZULA. ...You step over some invisible line you never even knew existed...

KACZMAREK. But I'm a *transparent* bastard...Yes – the wrong word at the wrong party to the wrong person...

ZULA. ...They rip your throat out.

WIKTOR. It's called freedom.

KACZMAREK (*mock exaltation*). We're free! Yes. Well, I love it. I'm sorry – the embassy said they'd be sending a car for me. Don't worry – I said to wait at the café on the corner. Driver likes to have a brandy – even first thing in the morning! Can you imagine? Strictly I was never here. You don't mind me running off.

ZULA. No.

KACZMAREK. It's wonderful to see you both again. I'm glad things have gone so well. I mean that. And listen, Wiktor, look, no hard feelings about what happened last time I saw you. In Berlin.

WIKTOR. No, I know.

KACZMAREK. I mean, I had the whole company to think of. I couldn't just...

WIKTOR. I know.

KACZMAREK. I wouldn't do it now. At least I don't think I would. I hope I wouldn't. Anyway, lovely to see you.

   KACZMAREK *kisses* ZULA *and shakes hands with* WIKTOR.

   I think about the old times often. All the time!

   He goes. WIKTOR *stands looking at their album cover, listening to the album play.*

ZULA. Proud of it?

WIKTOR. You don't like it, so I hate it. What can I say?

   She goes to him. He doesn't respond.

ZULA. It's all right. You can touch me.

WIKTOR. I do touch you.

ZULA. Not really. You talk in your sleep. But you never tell me anything.

WIKTOR. You're never interested in what I have to say.

ZULA. 'Cause you never say what I want to hear.

WIKTOR. Tell me what you want to hear.

ZULA. I want to hear you say everything you said before. That we can do whatever we like. That we can play whatever we like. Isn't that why we came here? Everything we've gone through and yet here we are, still rearranging the old music.

WIKTOR. Because I can't.

ZULA. Can't what?

WIKTOR. Compose music, write music.

ZULA. What are you talking about? Of course you can – you do!

WIKTOR. And I always hate it.

ZULA. But why?

WIKTOR. I don't know – I just do.

ZULA. But that's… Let me help you.

WIKTOR. I just can't do it. What can I say? I mean what can I…? I just can't fucking do it! So…

Silence.

I'm not sure I ever could. You regret coming after me.

ZULA. I don't know. It was worth finding out.

WIKTOR. Finding out what?

ZULA. Finding out if we weren't already dead when we met.

WIKTOR. We weren't dead. If anything, when I met you, it felt like I'd finally woken up.

ZULA. Mm. Maybe that's just a trick the devil played on us, the same trick he's been playing our whole lives. 'Yes – you're alive!' 'That's right! You have talent!' 'Run away!' 'Escape!' 'Go to Paris!' 'Make a record!' 'It's all so important!' But people like you and me – we're just two empty mirrors facing each other. The reflection looks like it's going somewhere, but it stretches away into nothing. 'Cause there's nothing there.

ZULA *puts on her coat. She leaves.* WIKTOR *sits there alone.*

WIKTOR. Zula?

Pause. He goes to the door.

Zula? (*He calls down the stairs.*) Zula?

Music plays.

AIMEE *comes and stands pouring some antiseptic on a cloth.* WIKTOR *moves towards a chair, his head hanging down, mopping blood from his face.*

AIMEE. Put your head back, let me see in the light.

WIKTOR *does as she instructs. She cleans his face.*

You're lucky. The bottle bounced off your eyebrow. Didn't break. Hold this on it.

WIKTOR *holds the cloth to his wound.* AIMEE *cleans up the rest of his face, his hands.*

WIKTOR. I'm sorry.

AIMEE. Really? You ask me, you goaded him till you got what you wanted.

WIKTOR. Mm.

AIMEE. Everybody thought you were some tramp. Where's that girl you were always with – at the clubs?

WIKTOR *shrugs.*

(*As she cleans* WIKTOR *up.*) I used to drink like that. I used to go into this place that opened in the early morning. They had a special licence to serve men who worked on the river. The men like big babies, leaning over the tables, crying, staggering about. There was this old woman who worked the place, she grabbed me one morning. 'What the hell are you doing in here?' she says to me. She got me to start thinking about my business. Think about taking care of myself.

WIKTOR. You were lucky.

AIMEE. Yeah! And you see you? The way you are now? You're gonna get killed. Maybe by accident. Maybe not – it's only a matter of... you know, the way you are, I mean. I wouldn't be shocked. I'm sorry to say it, but I won't be.

She considers his wound.

A wealthy client asked me to marry him the other night.

WIKTOR. You should do it.

AIMEE. I don't love him.

WIKTOR. Is that important?

AIMEE laughs.

AIMEE. You ask me that? Look what it's done to you.

WIKTOR. Listen, I've no money, but I... I mean if you...

AIMEE. You are joking? You absolutely stink. Go on. On your way.

The VICE CONSUL *of the Polish People's Republic comes in and stands at a window, looking over a file. On the wall, the Polish national emblem appears.*

WIKTOR *sits, his head hanging down.*

VICE CONSUL. All right. Here it is. You're not French, and you're not a Pole either. As far as we're concerned, according to this, you no longer exist. You're free. And between you and me... why on earth would you want to leave Paris?

WIKTOR. Because I'm Polish.

VICE CONSUL. Please, stop.

WIKTOR. I am.

VICE CONSUL. You ran away. You betrayed our country. That's not a small thing, Mr Zatoński. You let down all these young people who trusted you. You don't love Poland.

WIKTOR. I do.

VICE CONSUL. Hmph! This woman… (*Reads*.) Zuzanna
Lichoń. You two are not married.

WIKTOR. No.

VICE CONSUL. Says here she holds Italian citizenship. What
if she's gone there?

WIKTOR. I believe she's returned home. To Poland.

VICE CONSUL. Well, unfortunately, Mr Zatoński, if you want
my opinion you hold a very weak hand. I strongly advise you
not to play it. This is your file and right now, this person, in
here in this file? Returns to Poland? You'll die in prison.
They'll work you to death for what you did. *This* is what you
need to be thinking about, Mr Zatoński, this file and how to
make it look better.

WIKTOR. How?

VICE CONSUL. By showing us you love us. Don't look so
serious! We're in Paris. And everything is beautiful. You move
in artistic circles, you meet people, émigrés, even fellow
defectors I imagine. All you need to do is pop by, once a
month, tell us about these fellow birds of flight, how they're
getting on, how they're supporting themselves. For instance, if
they're getting a little assistance from the US Embassy
perhaps. If so, what kind of assistance. What do they offer in
return for this assistance? Nothing really, Mr Zantoński. Such
an easy way to show us you love us. It's nothing.

Once a month I send a report. Makes me look good. Makes
you look good. Everybody helps each other and who knows?
Time passes… I put in a positive word… Your file starts to
look a little less damning… Maybe a little trip home here
and there… to visit this, Miss Lichoń. Maybe. But you even
think of just returning home, to Poland, now? As *this* person?
(*He taps the file*.) Well… I'm afraid I can't help you.

WIKTOR *gets up to leave*.

One moment, Mr Zatoński, you're not quite free to go. Let me
just… make sure this information is accurate… (*Indicates
a bottle of liquor*.) Please help yourself to another. I never

touch it. (*Reads*.) Wiktor Zatoński – Father Paweł, Mother Julia, he was a dried-fruit importer. Away a lot. Your brother, Andrzej, dies of a brain haemorrhage in 1931 when you're twelve and he's thirteen. (*Clicks pen*.) That would be correct. Your father leaves on an extended business trip and you never see him again. You attend piano lessons with a Mr Leonid Bloom – that's right? But mostly you're a loner. You win a scholarship to the Fryderyk Chopin Conservatory of Music where you met Magdalena Abramowicz. Sort of a mentor to you, was she?

WIKTOR. She didn't think I was quite a virtuoso, but…

VICE CONSUL. She encouraged you.

WIKTOR. As I say… she didn't quite think I was as good as…

VICE CONSUL. …you thought you were. The war comes, our country is scorched to its very stones and somehow a piano-playing dandy about town such as yourself, seems to sail through it all without a scratch. It's a question mark that hangs about you everywhere you go, but it's no mystery really.

Because you found a rather special job, didn't you? Playing music at the Ziemiańska café. And if German officers came in to dine and if the Gestapo sat in the back and enjoyed your music, well – that was probably all the better. Because they liked you, Wiktor, don't they?

WIKTOR. I couldn't control who came in or out…

VICE CONSUL. Maybe but the point is – they *liked* you, Wiktor. Didn't they? You know they did. So you tinkled piano, night after night for the Nazis while your compatriots wasted and withered away all around you. German music. Beethoven, Bach and Wagner. They liked you so much you even played at their houses for their families, didn't you? Gave lessons to their children. But I mean… you had to live your life too, right? You're a good guy. And we were going to need good guys. Not hollowed-out wrecks. No. You needed to survive – your compositions needed to survive for God's sake! So – just no. Yep. And you lived. Well? Didn't you?

WIKTOR. Sort of.

VICE CONSUL. Hmm. We all survived somehow. You compromised then, Mr Zatoński. It's what you've always done. You are incapable of conviction. You know it, I know it. So don't look so glum. Because we all compromise now, Mr Zatoński. That's the price of belonging.

Love. Happens to us all at some time or other. But come on, there are a million French girls on every street corner down there. I mean – (*With disdain.*) one Polish girl…? You really want to go home and die in some forced labour camp to prove a point? You know that's not you. So. What's it to be?

WIKTOR *doesn't answer.*

Music delivers us to –

Poland, 1959.

A bare room. The sounds of rocks being broken. Distant shouts, gates clanking.

ZULA *is being searched by a* FEMALE GUARD *while an* OFFICER *reads her the rules concerning visits.*

The FEMALE GUARD *leaves. A* MALE GUARD *slumps in the corner, rifle on his lap, half-asleep.*

WIKTOR *is led into the room in shackles. He is shaven-headed, horrifically starved and bent over. Beaten. He trembles, blinking in the light. His right hand is disfigured.*

WIKTOR. Zula. You look terrible.

ZULA *can't help laughing.* WIKTOR *smiles a grimace – he's missing a front tooth.*

ZULA. How many years?

WIKTOR. Fifteen. Illegal border crossing in both directions. And it turns out I spied for the Americans too.

ZULA. What happened?

ZULA *takes* WIKTOR*'s disfigured hand and looks at it.*

WIKTOR. They made me pick.

ZULA. You chose the right?

WIKTOR *nods*.

But you're right-handed.

WIKTOR. I always preferred chords to melody. Melody gets me in trouble.

ZULA. You knew this would happen.

WIKTOR *nods*.

ZULA *takes a carton of cigarettes from her backpack and hands it to the* GUARD.

GUARD. Ten minutes.

He goes out.

ZULA. I brought you some food.

WIKTOR. Where are you living?

ZULA. A room in Kaczmarek's flat.

WIKTOR. Of course. How is he?

ZULA. He's fine. He sits and watches me every morning while I have my breakfast. Well in the afternoon. I never wake up till about twelve.

WIKTOR. He watches you.

ZULA. He pretends he isn't, but he stares at me from the other side of the apartment. While he organises bookings. He wants me to sing.

WIKTOR. Then you should.

ZULA (*shrugs*). I tried going home. But everything was... there was no one there. I went back to Warsaw. Kaczmarek sent me a ticket. He met me off the train and he kind of... proposed to me. Took me for a meal and offered me a sort of contract, but like, to marry him, to formalise my... to make things easier for his accountant.

WIKTOR. Did you say yes?

ZULA (*shakes her head*). I was going to come back to Paris.

WIKTOR *looks at her.*

I know. Then Kaczmarek told me you were... you were here.

WIKTOR. Stay with him.

ZULA (*shakes her head*). I can't. It'll kill me. In the long run.

WIKTOR. Something else will kill you in the long run anyway.
You have to hand it to him. He's been steadfast. My whole
life I have only ever done what's best for me.

ZULA. Doesn't everyone do that?

WIKTOR. I don't think so. Not everyone.

I never told you, I had a piano teacher. She was very kind to
me. In my first-year exam she told me I had an unusually
delicate touch. Too tentative. She offered to help me.

She was twenty years older than me, she was married, but
she and her husband lived in adjacent apartments so...
I began to spend a lot of time there.

ZULA. When was this?

WIKTOR. Thirties, late thirties. She even found me work.
When the Germans invaded Czechoslovakia her husband
was offered a residency at Princeton University. They were
Jewish, you see. And she offered to pay for me to join them.
But I felt things were just beginning to happen for me in
Warsaw and I told her... I couldn't. Told her she should go.
To tell you the truth, I also just kind of wished she would
go... because, you know...

Anyway she stayed. Probably for me. Her husband left. And
she... And the war came. And then all the Jews were ordered
into the... They were going to wall them all in.

ZULA (*nods*). Mm.

WIKTOR. Naturally, she didn't want to go. She gave me all of
her manuscripts to hide, Polish music and pieces that we
had worked on and I... Anyway, we snuck her into an

office. We hid her there, but down, two floors down under
the ground in a... kind of large... cupboard really behind a
septic tank. She was locked in there. It was safe, it was
sound-proof. But it was... Weeks went by like this. Then
someone from the faculty warned me that the building was
being watched and I just didn't... go there. I'd walk towards
that street, with some food in a little bundle, but I'd see a
car, or someone under a street lamp or I'd hear a voice in
the darkness and, any excuse, I'd just... turn round, and go
back to work. And play. Yeah. And I would hope that she
had... just, in the dark, just... She loved me. And I...
I took... it. And that is who I am. Just do me one favour,
will you? Find some normal man. An ordinary man with an
ordinary life.

She looks away. Silent for a moment.

ZULA. Guess what? I pray now.

WIKTOR. Yeah?

ZULA. I go into a church every night, round the corner from
Kaczmarek's flat. I even sit at the back at mass, sometimes.
Down the back.

They laugh.

WIKTOR. Okay.

ZULA. I sit there and wonder what kind of god watches us do
these things? All these horrible things, we do. Then I realised
maybe there is no god. Only a devil. It's the only thing that
makes sense.

WIKTOR *nods.*

I'll get you out of here, I promise.

Choral music fills the air – 'The Silent Child'.

ENSEMBLE.
Fixed to a broken tree
Have you forsaken me?
But if one is spared perhaps we all may be

Sleep now, my silent child
Sleep now, unusual boy
Sleep now, sleep now, sleep now…

WIKTOR *exits. Music fills the air.* ZULA *takes off her coat to reveal a sparkling dress covered in sequins. She performs 'He Taught Me To Lie':*

ZULA.
My love picked a poppy the colour of danger
The shade of fast kisses
The thrill of swift exchange
And I tell him everything
And what I don't know I just invent
That I've been faithless, that I've been scandalous
He stood by the wall with his ear to the glass
Imagining lovers as they pass
Imagining lovers we promised to be
While I pictured him kissing her, imagining me
'This is our little secret' I'd say under my breath
The distance from this life and death
He taught me well, he told me why, he taught me to lie.

Poland, 1964.

…A midnight summer festival. The song becomes a trashy mock-Latin pop pastiche.

WIKTOR *and* KACZMAREK *come through a backstage area, where* DANCERS *are doing quick-changes,* MUSICIANS *are tuning up.* ZULA *is grabbed by* DRESSERS *to do a quick change while the* BAND *continue onstage with a rousing cha-cha-cha…*

WIKTOR *is dressed in an old suit. His hair is entirely grey. His injured hand is held awkwardly against his body.*

KACZMAREK *is a little fatter and balding, but on the whole looks well, in a grey suit and thick-rimmed glasses. A* NANNY *stands with him, holding a baby in a basket with a handle…* KACZMAREK *watches proudly for a moment – he sings along.*

KACZMAREK (*loudly over the music*). Can you believe it?
  Zula actually says she hates music now!! Isn't that funny?
  She'll be very pleased to see you, Wiktor! You'll cheer her
  up! She doesn't quite realise it – but coming home was the
  best decision she ever made. Because Polish people
  understand her. These festival crowds especially – when her
  voice is in better nick I mean – she's tired. You can hear it.
  She struggles a little of course because the music is louder
  nowadays! You have to go with it. It's the sixties! We're not
  warbling the old folk tunes now, Wiktor! But her feeling –
  her sentiment, let's face it – it's sentimentality – but in
  popular music that's what people want, right? That's what
  it's all about! I'm glad to see you, Wiktor. It's nice of you to
  find the time.

  The NANNY *rocks the baby as wails emit from the basket.*
  KACZMAREK *takes the basket.*

  Don't be sad, Piotruś. Come, introduce yourself. This is
  Piotruś.

  WIKTOR *looks into the basket.*

WIKTOR. Hello.

KACZMAREK (*shouting over the noise*). He keeps waking up!
  Do we look alike?

WIKTOR. He's your spitting image.

KACZMAREK. You think so? Everybody tells me he's like
  Zula – but not at all like me! Do you want to hold him?

WIKTOR. No, it's fine.

KACZMAREK (*to the* NANNY, *brusquely*). Here! Come here!
  Where are you going? Take him back to the hotel – his
  mother will be finished performing in an hour.

  The NANNY *leaves with the basket.*

  So? Will you get back to music?

  WIKTOR *shows* KACZMAREK *his misshapen right hand,
  which is trembling a little.*

WIKTOR. I can't play.

KACZMAREK. Don't let that stop you. You still have one good
hand – that's all you need to arrange – to compose – and that
one – Well, you can conduct with it! Long as you can hold
a baton, right? You could even stick one on it!

He waves his hand about.

I'm joking.

WIKTOR *smiles. Someone brings them drinks. They stand
awkwardly with their drinks for a few moments.*

Look, I'm just glad we were able to get you out of there.
It wasn't easy. But the deputy minister is our neighbour, and
a good friend. And you know Zula when she puts her mind
to something. What did you do in the end? Three years?

WIKTOR. Five.

KACZMAREK. Five. That's right. Yes. Well. Could have been
a lot more. Could have been worse.

WIKTOR. Thank you. I'm really grateful.

KACZMAREK. I love that record you did in Paris. It's so good.
Wonderful arrangements. But it would be better to record it
again – here, in Polish. Zula could use that. And so could
you. Think about it.

WIKTOR *nods.* **ZULA** *has finished her set to cheering and
applause.*

Oh! Here she comes. Wait till she sees you!

ZULA *comes stumbling offstage towards them and falls.*
KACZMAREK *catches* **ZULA.**

Not like this, darling. Not here. Where's your tablets? Ha ha
ha! Look who's here!

ZULA *sits on the floor.* **WIKTOR** *and* **ZULA** *look at each
other in silence.*

Sorry, Wiktor, give me a hand, would you? No pun intended!

WIKTOR *helps* KACZMAREK *to get* ZULA *up.*

Eh? Ha ha! These tablets she's taking for her voice! I never know if she's had too many or too few! It's impossible! And you simply cannot drink on top of them, which is… Oh look. Can I introduce you to Kelvin and Kelva? They're up next.

WIKTOR *waves to a* YOUNG MAN *and* YOUNG WOMAN *in sparkly costumes holding guitars, waiting to go onstage.*

I look after them. They write all their own material. Pop songs, ballads. Don't they look marvellous? People like you and Zula paved the way you know. Zula? You need a cup of coffee that's all! They'll bring you one. (*To* WIKTOR.) The deputy minister is coming to say hello. I'd invite you, Wiktor, but… ha ha ha…

WIKTOR. No, that's fine.

KACZMAREK (*looks around*). Where's the…? One second, I need to see where our bloody driver is! Wiktor, do me a favour, and don't let her drink anything, will you? (*To* ZULA.) Don't drink tonight, darling, we have to be up early to catch our plane in the morning. I'll see you both in a minute.

WIKTOR *and* ZULA *look at one another.* ZULA *takes off her wig.*

ZULA. Can you get me out of here?

ZULA *rests her head on* WIKTOR's *shoulder. He holds her close. They close their eyes and stay like that for a long time.*

Everything changes around them. The artifice of the theatre show is gone.

They are on a bare stage with bare light. We feel as though we are also in this light. We are all in the same space. It's silent.

WIKTOR *helps* ZULA. *He puts her coat on her and fixes her hair. They look like two vagrants. They look old. They come to a bench and sit looking out.*

ZULA *takes a bottle with some pills. They both take a handful. It's silent.* ZULA *takes a stump of a candle from her pocket, sticks it on the bench and lights it. Dusk is falling.*

ZULA. I, Wiktor Zatoński, take you, Zuzanna Lichoń, to be my wife.

WIKTOR. I, Wiktor Zatoński, take you, Zuzanna Lichoń, to be my wife.

ZULA. And I swear to be with you always, until death do us part.

WIKTOR. And I swear to be with you always, until death do us part.

ZULA. I, Zuzanna Lichoń, take you, Wiktor Zatoński, to be my husband. And I swear to be with you always until death do us part. So help us God.

ZULA *looks at* WIKTOR *and crosses herself. He does the same. She gives him a few more pills.*

More for you. You're heavier.

They swallow the pills.

She sings softly.

There's a tree at the crossroads
There's a nail in my shoe
Repeat to me softly
As you vow that we'll see it through…
Let's go to the other side
And take in the view
Our eyes will see better there
Watching the river flow
You may say I don't know, but I do…

A distant accompaniment, maybe a hurdy-gurdy, can be heard somewhere. WIKTOR *sings quietly along with her. His voice hoarse and unsteady.*

WIKTOR.
Every night will be starless
Every day will be fine

Each hour will be peaceful
As the reeds make the river slow…

ZULA *and* WIKTOR.

The earth will be broken
And we'll lie there alone
I am yours you are mine
To long for longer is a crime
You may say I don't lie
But I do, But I do…

WIKTOR. What do you think will happen?

ZULA. Well, we either go straight to Hell, which I imagine is kind of empty. Or Purgatory, which I'm kind of used to. Or Heaven. Maybe it's already happened. If I'm here with you.

Maybe this is it. And everything is exactly as it's supposed to be. All the pain in the world. It has to be the way it is, because we have to suffer. In order to – (*Shrugs.*) understand.

WIKTOR. Understand what?

ZULA. How lucky we are.

They sit there watching the wind blow through the trees.

Everything fades away.

The End.

ALMEIDA
THEATRE

The Almeida Theatre makes brave new work that asks big questions: of plays, of theatre and of the world around us. Whether new work or reinvigorated classics, the Almeida brings together the most exciting artists to take risks; to provoke, inspire and surprise our audiences.

Since 2013, the Almeida has been led by Artistic Director Rupert Goold and Executive Director Denise Wood.

Recent highlights include Jeremy Herrin's production of Sam Holcroft's *A Mirror*; Almeida Associate Director Rebecca Frecknall's Olivier Award-winning production of *A Streetcar Named Desire*; Rupert Goold's productions of Peter Morgan's *Patriots* (all transferred to the West End), and *Tammy Faye*, a new musical from Elton John, Jake Shears and James Graham (transfers to Broadway in 2024).

Previous productions include Rupert Goold's productions of Steven Sater and Duncan Sheik's *Spring Awakening* (also screened in cinemas UK wide), James Graham's *Ink* (transferred to the West End and Broadway) and Mike Bartlett's *King Charles III* (transferred to the West End and Broadway and adapted for BBC television); Rebecca Frecknall's Olivier Award-winning production of Tennessee Williams' *Summer and Smoke* (transferred to the West End); Robert Icke's productions of *Hamlet* and *Oresteia* (both of which transferred to New York) and *Mary Stuart* (West End and UK tour); and Lyndsey Turner's Olivier Award-winning production of Lucy Kirkwood's *Chimerica*.

www.nickhernbooks.co.uk

facebook.com/nickhernbooks

twitter.com/nickhernbooks